A GIRL SCARRED:

A JOURNEY TO OVERCOMING

SHANEIL MCGAWN-FRANCIS

PUBLISHED BY:

Yahweh's Anointed Publishing
where your writing comes to life, one page at a time.

A GIRL SCARRED: A JOURNEY TO OVERCOMING
Written by Shaneil McGawn-Francis
Copyright © 2019 by Shaneil McGawn-Francis

All scripture quotations, unless otherwise indicated, are taken from the Holy Bible. Scripture quotations are from the King James Version (KJV), New Living Translation (NLT), New Kings James Version (NKJV) and the New International Version (NIV) and are indicated.

ISBN: **978-976-96427-0-6**

Cover Art Designed by: GEEK RESOURCE CENTRE geekjamaica@gmail.com

Edited by: The Research Centre wen_dionne@yahoo.com

Published by:

Yahweh's Anointed Publishing
Tel: 876-549-0063/876-438-2256
Email: yahwehsanointedpublishing@gmail.com

DEDICATION

My heart's desire and passion is to see the lives of people transformed.

I dedicate this book to you as you travel on your journey in life, be encouraged that your start does not determine your ending.

There is always hope for a better tomorrow.

Though the road may be rocky, you will get where you are going because you are not alone.

TABLE OF CONTENTs

ACKNOWLEDGEMENTS

I first of all bless the Lord for choosing me as His vessel to produce this book, which will no doubt be instrumental in the transformation of the lives of people.

I thank my husband, Hamphroy Francis for his encouragements and for being my tower of strength for fourteen years. I say hats off to him for his support as I wrote this book. Thank you my cheerleader!

I extend special gratitude to Bishop Courtney McLean, my spiritual father for his encouragement and guidance over the years. I thank him for constantly checking the progress of this book and motivating me along the way.

Thanks to my friends Popsann Lambert-Francis and Annakay Williams for their encouragements and prayers. Thanks to Minister Clatin Williams and Dionne Smith for their reviews and words of encouragement. To all who have helped me one way or another on this journey, I thank you.

FOREWORD

Shaneil McGawn-Francis is one of my spiritual daughters at Worship and Faith International Fellowship, whose spiritual and personal transformation I have personally witnessed over the years. As such I am pleased to be writing the Forward for this book. She is faithful, diligent and is fully aware of the call of God that is on her life which is reflected in the book you are now holding in your hand.

A Girl Scarred: A Journey to Overcoming will take you on a life transformational journey as it progressively highlights the life of another and how she overcame. As you read with an open mind, be reassured that your past hurt doesn't have to be a hindrance to you having a purposeful life. Be encouraged to move ahead and achieve all that you desire. You were not born to be stagnated by your challenges but they should be a springboard for you to push even harder.

Shaneil has written this book out of her past experiences with the goal of providing a tool that will help others to overcome irrespective of what they have been through. Shaneil is qualified to do so because her life is the epitome of restoration after being abused, hurt and broken. Despite the challenges, she has learnt how to emerge as a victor over her past.

It is easy for persons to use their life challenges as an excuse for not living at their full potential but do not let that be you. You were born to represent Jesus Christ in this earth. You will complete this book with a renewed mind.

Bishop Courtney McLean
Founder and Senior Pastor
Worship and Faith International Fellowship (WAFIF)
Jamaica and Fort Lauderdale
Author: Lessons on Demonology Volume 1
       Honouring God the Gateway to Success
       Turning Nothing into Something

INTRODUCTION

A Girl Scarred: A Journey to Overcoming was written with inspiration from the Holy Spirit. As you turn the pages of this book you will be delving into the intriguing and captivating life of a girl who grew up in humble beginnings. She was abused, became heartbroken and suicidal but by God's grace was able to overcome. As you flip through the pages, becoming acquainted with the life story of another, get ready for a shift to take place in your mind and by extension your life. A transformed life is as a result of a transformed mind. It is not where you are or where you have been that matters, it is where you are going.

CHAPTER ONE: EARLY DAYS

As Gloria sat quietly on her veranda gazing into the distance and listening to the wind blowing softly in the cool evening of summer, she was brought back to her early days when she lived with her grandmother. She remembered the smell of the sweet aroma of her grandma's world famous potato pudding baking on the old iron coal stove that was placed at the door of the small kitchen to allow her to check on it. Other memories from her childhood flashed across her mind bringing her back to a simpler time. A time when the greatest challenge she had was deciding which game to play.

Those days were filled with laughter as the children, filled with bottomless energy played various games in front of the old wooden house that was the resident of the **"Mason's"** family. The neighbours' children would trickle into the big yard to play a game of either football, cricket, dandy shandy, or marbles. Seated on the wide verandah, some on porch chairs, others on the steps, were the older folks, who seemed to be enjoying the entertainment provided by the children as they played.

Gloria remembered not having one of the most basic human necessities back then – electricity - but she was comfortable in her little world. Though many of her neighbours were privileged to have their ironing done with an electric iron, Gloria had no such experience. Her ironing was done by using a cast iron welded together to resemble an electric iron. The iron was then placed on hot coals. Once it was hot, it was removed and used to iron out their Sunday best for church and school uniforms. She remembered walking to Miss May's shop to buy 'suck suck' [a homemade juice that came in little plastic bags] or to beg her neighbours cold water to cool her down on hot summer days. Granny didn't like her bothering the neighbours. Even though the neighbours were willing to assist her and would offer her the use of their refrigerator to store her meat she never did. Granny often said she '*was content in her condition*' and would instead hang the meats outside after first preserving them with salt.

Another fond memory Gloria had was that of making the fire needed to prepare meals as they did not own a gas or an electric stove. She remembered using either coals or wood to start the fire. This was an exciting task for her to do. She remembered carefully selecting the coals or wood to place in a pile, then sprinkling kerosene oil all over the coals. A plastic bag was then lit with a lighter and placed over the coals to get the fire started. Fire droplets from the plastic bag would ignite the coals/woods. On the few occasions when the trick of using plastic bags didn't work, Gloria had to put her face down to the pile, which was now filled with smoke to blow on it to get the fire blazing. If that didn't work a thick cardboard, the cover from an old notebook or newspaper folded together was used to fan the pile vigorously until the flames appeared.

Gloria coughed as though the smoke she was remembering had somehow found its way into her lungs at that particular moment. Gloria sighed and closed her eyes, losing herself to her memories before the loud barking of the neighbour's dogs jerked her out of her reverie. The sound of the dog barking reminded her of the horrific experience she had that changed her life dramatically for years. The memory of a dog's wet tongue sliding across her face was floating through her mind as she recalled what happened.

"Horrible," she whispered. She shook herself as if to shake away the memory then got up from the chair and walked to the kitchen to get a glass of water. As she walked back to the veranda and began drinking the water

her thoughts turned to the many times in her youth she used a bucket to fetch water from the well in the back yard or from the neighbours pipe three houses down. Bottles of water had to be filled from the pipe for drinking and the well water was used for bathing and sometimes cooking and washing. Being small and skinny, it was quite nerve racking for Gloria to stand over the well, not being able to see the water level, but having to toss the bucket in to get the water. Then she had to pull the rope up from the dark hole and poured the water into the waiting container placed on the ground nearby. After the vessel was filled, she walked with it back to her house and poured it into a tub that was kept outside. It would stay there all night until Gloria woke up and was ready to take her morning bath for school.

By morning the water was icy cold as it was left opened to the night elements. She giggled a bit at the thought of how quickly she would bathe because the water was so cold. Often times she was done bathing without even a speck of water touching her back. The memory brought laughter to Gloria's lips as she remembered those mornings with joy.

****

Gloria loved reading and always had a book in her hand. She was ecstatic when she was allowed to borrow up to three books from the community library. She was very mature for her age and wanted to read *Mills and Boon* and other romance novels that she saw her older cousin reading. Once per week, Gloria went to the library and borrowed three books. She would hurry home to start reading because of the constant warnings she was given not to be reading while walking. By the end of the week she would be finished reading all of them.

Gloria easily lost herself in the world of the books she was reading. Hours would go by without her moving. The sound of her mother yelling her name to come inside would bring her back to reality. She would slowly stagger from where she was seated and head towards the dinner table where the lamp was placed. She sat near to the lamp so she could finish the adventure she was reading. She hated having to put down the book when it was getting more interesting with the turn of each page. She could be so deeply wrapped up into a novel that she didn't even pay attention to the fact that she was moving the book closer and closer to her eyes as the lamp flames dimmed occasionally, resulting in her being unable to see the words on the page easily.

She was abruptly dragged from the world she was in as her mom pulled the book from her hand with a stern warning that she would set herself on fire if she continued to put her face so close to the flames. Disappointment flooded her as she went off to bed eagerly awaiting the rising sun that would provide sufficient light for her to continue her reading. While drifting off to sleep, Gloria thought how different things would be if she had electricity. All the other houses close to hers sparkled with lights and the sound of merriment as they watched television or listened to the radio…but hers didn't.

****

Gloria was brought back to present-day as a cool breeze blew across her face and with it the delicious smell of someone's sumptuous meal of curried chicken. Gloria's tongue swept across her mouth and she suddenly realized she was hungry.

"That must be Miss Mazy cooking," she said, glancing in the direction of her closest neighbour.

She hurriedly got up and headed inside. She warmed some leftover food she had in the refrigerator and sat down in front of the television to watch a movie as she ate. It meant a lot to Gloria that she was now able to live like this which was the opposite to what she encountered in the earlier years of her life. As she glanced at the images moving across the television set, the memory of her days without television came to her mind. She smiled as she remembered the nights when everyone, her siblings and cousins included, would go to the neighbour's house to watch their favourite sitcoms and occasionally a few horror movies. When it was time to return home, they were very afraid. They all huddled together and walked as quickly as they could along the dark path until they reached the safety of their home.

****

Gloria loved to attend school. However, her father was not around to assist her mother. She was left to care for five children by herself. Living in a single income home meant Gloria could only attend school two or three days each week and sometimes not at all. Despite her circumstances she was desperate to fulfil her dream of becoming a doctor. On the request of her mother she would sometimes need to borrow money from neighbours or relatives even though she was embarrassed to do so. At times her mother insisted that they all stayed home because there was no money and she refused to borrow anymore. Gloria always cried thinking of how much she was missing out on in not going to school, but she had no choice. Gloria, as well as her teachers were worried about how her grades were falling due to her irregular attendance to school. Being aware of her situation and in an effort to help her, the school added her to the 'School's Feeding Programme' that would provide her with free lunch every day she was in school. While that took care of lunch there was still the challenge of finding the bus fare needed to travel the 12 miles to school. Gloria was goal driven and she was destined to fulfil her dreams and to one day be called Dr. Gloria Mason. With this at the forefront of her mind she promised herself that she was going to take matters into her own hands.

On days when there was no money, she walked to her relatives houses and asked for bus fare. Sometimes she only received enough to get to school. Not worried about how she would return home, Gloria went to school. She studied hard and spent most of her days in the school library. The thought of not having the bus fare to return home would only resurface at dismissal. Nevertheless, she always got the money required whether by a classmate, teacher or a free ride on the bus. She hated having to depend on others but she had no choice. It was either that or stay at home and watch her dream become more challenging to achieve with the passing of each day she was out of school. People were judgmental towards her as they were not cognizant of her struggles. But

God's favour was upon her and she managed to always reached back home safely.

Some days Gloria felt discouraged and low-spirited as she thought of how difficult things were for her family. She often felt alone and ashamed. One such day was when the time came for her to pay her examination fees. As the due date inched closer for the final payment she was a bundle of nerves as she did not have nor did she know where the money would come from to pay for her examinations. Quietly she walked to a section of the school where no one could see her and cried. She felt hopeless. In her desperation she offered up a prayer to God, begging Him to send help for her.

After a few minutes a classmate of hers walked up and asked if she was ok. Gloria quickly said "*yes*" because even at the verge of death on the inside, she always said she was fine and managed to force a smile on her face. Her classmate was determined and stood with her silently as she pulled herself together. She would not budge. She enquired if Gloria was worried about the examinations fees. Bashfully, Gloria nodded "*yes*". She took Gloria to the guidance counsellor and explained her situation to her. Gloria got the help she needed. Arrangements were made for Gloria to repay the money after she left school.

There were certain situations in her life that shaped her into the woman she would become and that was one of them.

Despite all of those happenings in her early years, people thought she had everything handed to her. But Oh, how wrong they were. No one truly knows the struggles of others unless they are told. Imagine a girl at the age of fifteen, whose sole responsibility at that age should be to focus on school and being a child but instead she had to be thinking about how she was going to finance her education, get needed resources among other things. These situations sometimes lead young girls to make foolish choices that ultimately lead to problems. Given Gloria's situation, her life could have taken a different turn. After all, she was propositioned several times by numerous men that were old enough to be her father. They would offer gifts but she was smart enough to know that if she took their gifts she would be required to reciprocate and that was **NOT** going to happen. So she never took anything they offered. Even when she had nothing at all, she learned to *'be content in whatever state she found herself'* a lesson she had learnt from her grandmother. Like most of her peers, she also had a boyfriend but he was not aware of how bad things were for her. She kept it to herself. She made a decision not to take anything from him even when he offered.

Gloria did not enjoy the latter part of her adolescent years. She was not able to do many of the things her peers were doing due to money always being in short supply in her home. But she didn't care much about that. She was destined for greatness and greatness was what she was seeking after. She knew she was meant to be somebody so she refused to be distracted by her present state. Her desperate will to accomplish greatness was her motivator. Attached to that desperation came hard work, focus, intrinsic motivation, endurance and inner strength.

"Inner strength, right," she thought with a cold smirk on her face.

On several occasions she doubted very much if she had inner strength based on the number of times she cried or questioned why she had such colossal struggles. But before it got better it would get worse. Little did Gloria know that the difficulties of her childhood were nothing compared to what was to come. Her darkest days were still ahead of her…

CHAPTER TWO: GLOOM DAY

Gloria's heart rate increased as she remembered the night her little world began unravelling around her. All the fond memories of her childhood were beginning to fade from her mind. She felt out of breath, hurt, broken and angry as the memory of her past hurt hovered over her head, trampling all other thoughts in an effort to come to the forefront. Gloria clenched her fist as the day suddenly felt as though it was passing by at the speed of light. She felt outside of herself as tears ran down her face freely. Gloria shook her head vigorously, hoping that the dreaded memory would somehow disappear from her mind. She tried, but there it was creeping to the front of her mind.

D-Day - August 5, 2004

It was a dark, cold and lonely night. The howls of dogs and the chirping of birds were the only sounds that filled the atmosphere. Gloria walked down the dirt track hugging herself as she softly hummed with fear in her voice. She walked briskly, trying to get to her destination as quickly as possible. A dog dashed across her path making her jumped in fright. Gloria continued walking. The return journey seemed to take longer than she thought it should but she kept walking hoping she would get to her destination soon. By the time she realized she was not alone it was too late.

She never heard him. She didn't know which direction he came from. He never made a sound. The only time she knew he was there was when he grabbed her from behind. He flung her to the ground. Fear swept through her as she realized what was about to happen. She opened her mouth to scream for help but was quickly stopped by a very masculine hand clamped over her mouth.

Gloria felt helpless. She kicked feverishly as she felt her skirt being lifted. Her eyes widened in fear and pain as she felt the first thrust of what would take away her innocence and introduce a new kind of fear into her world. Gloria could no longer hear, see, smell, or feel as all her senses seemed to have stopped working. She laid still as he continued to move. In between blinks, all she could see was darkness all around her. Once he was finished, the figure ran off. She couldn't find the strength to move and so she laid there with tears streaming down her cheeks. She was flabbergasted with what just happened to her.

Gloria was only sixteen and had never been intimate with a man before. She thought about what she had lost and the pain became too much for her to bear. She curled into a ball and stared down the dirt track that had become her bed. She was bought back to her painful reality by the wet strokes of a dog's tongue on her face. She could not believe what had just happened to her. With great effort she managed to pull herself up from the ground and ran her hands along her legs. They were filled with blood. Despite the pain she was feeling, she had a sudden burst of energy that allowed her to pick her slippers off the ground and ran all the way home.

The days following the incident were difficult for Gloria. She remembered the fear that ate at her inside. Fear for what she lost and fear of people finding out. She didn't think she could live with herself if anyone found out what took place that night. She believed people would look at her differently, including her family. So she kept it hidden.

Gloria turned to writing poems and songs, which helped to keep her mind off that horrific night. Days passed. Followed by weeks and months. But Gloria was hurting with every passing minute. She wasn't healing. The pain seemed to increase rather than decrease. The more pain she felt, the more Gloria's thoughts became dark.

"This is it. I would rather to be dead than to face this pain," she thought on several occasions with a knife to her wrist.

Gloria was not the girl she was before the incident. She was in a very dark place and thought there was no way to find her way back. Her grades were falling and it was very difficult for her to concentrate in class. Her days became nights and her nights became days as she grappled with the pain of being sexually abused.

With each flashback to that night, she wanted to end her life. *"How can I live with this pain I am feeling? Isn't it better I am dead?"* Gloria thought with a tear stained face and a knife at her wrist. The knife went through the outer layers of her skin but due to its dullness it did not cut as deeply as Gloria wanted it to. Nonetheless, blood ran from her hand and she watched with anger steaming through her like the flames from the wood fires she lit in her younger years. Gloria felt dead even though she was alive. She knew what her dreams were but with the constant dull feelings she felt, she had pushed them to the back of her mind.

One day while in class, she felt so burdened and her heart ached to the point where she felt as though she was going to burst. Gloria ran from the class with tears pouring down her face and stood in a corner close to her classroom. Gloria turned to the only person she thought could help her – God. She cried to Him with such anger and bitterness as she asked God why. *Why did this happen to me? Why me Lord? What have I ever done wrong? I thought I was living a good life?* She begged God to send help for her now. As she stood there a hand touched her shoulder and a lady questioned, *"Are you ok? Why are you crying? Is something wrong?"*

Gloria did not answer but continued to cry.

The lady finally asked, *"Did someone hurt you?"*

All Gloria could do was nod her head. And with that, relief crept through her body. The lady took her to the guidance counsellor. Gloria didn't know who the lady was. It was the first and last time she saw her. When Gloria reflected on that day, she believed it was a guardian angel sent by God in answer to her desperate prayers as she never laid eyes on her again after that day.

Initially the visits to the counsellor's office did not reap much results because Gloria refused to open up. She felt that she would be judged and gossiped about. She trusted no one. Eventually the sessions started to reap more results because she became more comfortable with the counsellor. Many times she did not like going because the counselling sessions forced her to recall what she went through and how it made her feel.

Gloria was afraid to face the realization that not opening up would only prevent her from getting the help she needed. Despite the counselling sessions, Gloria sometimes returned to a dark place. This was seen in her attitude and behaviour. The door to suicidal thoughts opened up to her when she thought the pain was too much to bear. She felt she had no support system and this caused her to feel even more trapped in her painful world.

One morning Gloria got up late and realized she was alone in the house. Her mom and siblings were nowhere in sight. It was the day after a counselling session which had left her feeling hurt all over again. She felt hopeless and worthless. Thoughts of how much it was her fault plagued her mind. She felt like she had had enough of the pain that someone had forced on her. A young, innocent girl longing for the love and support of a loved one but none was near. She longed for the embrace of a parent or a friend. She hoped that someone could see that she was suffering on the inside and help her but they were all oblivious to her pain. She was crying out for help but the world seemed to be cut off from her. This was no ordinary feeling for her. It was torture. She couldn't bear it. She just couldn't. She walked around daily as if she was doing perfectly fine but deep inside, she felt as though she was carrying a big stone that was constantly weighing her down.

The morning she was left alone she thought, *"Today is the day. I am tired of this feeling"*.

With that thought in mind and tears flowing down her cheeks, Gloria sat on the bathroom floor with all her mom's medications next to her. Quickly, she emptied the contents from all the bottles, threw some in her mouth and swallowed. Just as she was about to throw the rest of the pills in her mouth they were swatted out of her hand and scattered all over the bathroom floor. Before she could look up, her younger brother bellowed,
"Are you an idiot? What are you doing?"

Gloria cried even harder and said, ***"Leave me alone let me die".***

With that she put her hand filled with more pills to her mouth. Her brother grabbed her hand and he too began to cry. They both sat there on the bathroom floor in silence as tears trickled down their small faces. Her brother didn't ask why she wanted to kill herself and she didn't say. Gloria suddenly felt sleepy and walked to the bedroom. As she drifted off to sleep with tears still running down her cheeks she thought, *"I finally did it. This is it. The end to my pain."* Life as she knew it was over for her and she was now going to die. With that final thought she closed her eyes.

Gloria was awakened by the sound of her mom's loud voice. She was very upset when her brother told her what Gloria had tried to do. In disappointment, she slowly closed her eyes, sighed and went back to sleep when she realized she was not dead. Sometime later she was awaken by her mom's voice once again. This time there was concern in her voice as Gloria had been sleeping for two whole days. When Gloria heard this she was in disbelief.

"Two days?" Gloria thought. *"There must be something out there that is bigger than I am. Who is not ready for*

me to leave this world because everything I tried to get rid of this painful life, has failed."

Gloria's mother was saddened by what Gloria did but did not say much on the matter. Her siblings also knew but no one said anything. The next few days became quite uncomfortable for her because the household became very quiet. Gloria withdrew herself from everyone and mostly spent her time writing poems and songs. She shut herself away from her family and friends as she became deeply depressed.

Sunday morning came and everyone got ready to go to church, except Gloria. She had stopped attending church after the incident happened in an effort to distance herself from God, on whom she placed some of the blame for allowing the abuse to happen to her. Gloria was very angry with God. She had been a Christian for years when the incident happened. The other person she blamed was herself because if she had not left her house that night and was walking alone nothing would have happened to her. Her mother shouted, interrupting her thoughts, *"No one is staying in this house this morning, we are all going to church."* Reluctantly Gloria got ready for church.

In church that morning Gloria sat absent-mindedly skimming the congregation and not listening to what the preacher was saying. Her mom touched her and signaled for her to go up for prayer. At this point Gloria realized that preaching had ended and it was that time in the service where persons go to the altar to have others pray with them. Gloria felt pinned to her seat as she watched several persons file to the altar to stand with their head bowed and eyes closed. She looked in her mother's direction and noticed her giving her the side eye [which meant get up there or else..]. Gloria got up from her seat and walked hesitantly to the front. After a few minutes, Gloria felt a hand on her shoulder and she opened her eyes. Right in front of her stood the preacher. He removed the microphone from his mouth and said,

"God said to tell you that anything you try in an effort to take your life will not work. He is not ready for you as yet because you have purpose to fulfill and until that is done you will remain here."

With tears running down her cheeks she thought about what the preacher had said and wondered how he knew that she had attempted to take her life. She was amazed. Did God really send him to tell her that? If yes, it means He heard her prayers. The very thought changed Gloria's outlook on life from that day. She now had a new look on life that took her mind off wanting to end her life. She now knew that God had not abandoned her like her father did. He was still her God who had heard her desolate cries for answers. While Gloria still did not understand why her, she felt a little better having received the word from the preacher that God knows her and sees what she was going through. It was enough to change her – for now.

****

The effects of the rape had changed Gloria. Gloria became hateful towards men and didn't want anything to do with them. After a while she found herself so deep in pain that she could no longer feel anything. It's almost as though her emotions were frozen solid. In addition to wanting to end her life Gloria became bitter. She hated everyone around her including herself. She started hurting the people around her with her words.

When someone is victimized they either internalize the pain or externalize it. Gloria did both. Prior to the abuse, Gloria loved looking in the mirror as she was fascinated with herself. At this point though, Gloria could not look at herself in the mirror unless it was to say "I hate you." This she did because she blamed herself for what had happened to her. She was doing it out of the pain she was experiencing.

Gloria was a beautiful and smart girl and of course guys were attracted to her. But who would have thought that a girl who hated men so much would have given herself to them after such a tragic event.

****

Gloria spend many hours thinking about it and finally came to the conclusion that all men wanted was sex. Gloria conditioned her mind to give them what they wanted in exchange for the morsel of love they gave her in return that she used to satisfy her need for the love she so desperately craved. She opened up herself to anyone that showed her the slightest expression of love but they were few and far between. For though she searched for people to love her, she could not love them in return and so the relationships did not last.

Gloria managed to have relationships but she could not love the guys she dated and sometimes she was dating up to four guys at a time. Gloria was looking for something that no man could give to her, but she did not know that. She was promiscuous to the point where she wondered if she was a prostitute without pay. She wanted to stop but couldn't, and so the hunt continued and the result was more hurt added to her current pain. It was quite evident to her that the men did not want her but instead wanted what she so freely offering to them.

Gloria also thought that in spite of her beauty, once a man was pursuing her, she felt she had to give him what he wanted before he took it by force. She knew she was in a dark place, but she didn't trust anyone to help her out of it. She kept everything bottled inside her. After every sexual escapade, she felt cheap, dirty and used. She spent many lonely days crying and thinking of how to kill herself. But she belonged to God. She was still His. The prophecy from the pastor was at the back of her mind and it kept Gloria going and made her believe she would smile again. The length of time she would have to wait was not clear, but the fact that she was promised a better life, she just had to wait it out.

CHAPTER THREE: ROAD TO RECOVERY

The road to recovery was the roughest. All the hurt and pain that afflicted her mind for years would not be easy to fix. Have you ever had something broken to the point where you think it could not be fixed? Maybe you even thought of throwing it away and getting a new one, but it was something you cherished and so you tried your endeavour best to mend it? Material things can be replaced or mended immediately, but emotional trauma can take a very long time to heal. Gloria learnt that lesson the hard way.

The healing of emotional hurt and pain is dependent on the process the individual goes through. It is not like a television movie where you can change the channel and the movie is changed and is no more. Memories are not like that. They are always there, but will be concealed when other things take precedence in your life. Gloria felt emotionally dead, lost, broken and hopeless. Sometimes the pain was so fierce that she would just sit and cry for hours or gaze off into space. Gloria's initial visits to the counsellor's office were just the beginning of what it would take for her to overcome the unpleasant memory of the sexual abuse, but it served as a start to getting her to open up to others.

After a few visits to the counsellor, Gloria began to share her experience with new friends she met. The more she spoke about it, the emptier and at peace she felt. Talking to others about it was a suggestion from her counsellor. She advised her to find trusted people to share what had happened to her. This was therapeutic for Gloria. The more she shared her story, the easier it became to tell others and the more healed she felt. After a while it was so easy to talk about it but even that in itself was a journey in perseverance as she visited counsellor after counsellor before she found the one she could share her trauma with openly.

Gloria remembered her painful journey throughout the years as she visited one counsellor after another. As much as how she needed the pain to go away, she hated visiting the counsellor because of the toll it took on her emotions. But which is worst? Getting the help you need despite the pain or not getting any help and constantly living in pain? Because Gloria blamed herself for what had happened to her it kept her in a prison of her own making. In one of her counselling sessions she told the counsellor that it was her fault and maybe she deserved it. The counselor reassured her that it was typical for persons who have been assaulted or abused to feel that it was their fault but it was not.

"How can a rape be the victims fault? Nobody would ask for such pain," she would say in her calm melodic voice.

"The victim did not ask to be raped," she repeated silently to herself.

Someone had robbed Gloria of something that was hers to give to her husband and this was something very difficult for her to accept. Many persons go through situations in their lives and instead of getting the help needed they often lean to their own understanding, which often present a warp view of things. Thus rather than getting better they often get worst. Rather than healing, they perpetuate the cycle and begin hurting others and themselves.

Monstrous thoughts of that night tormented Gloria's mind constantly throughout the years. The flashbacks were like a disease eating at her thoughts and emotions. They would leave her feeling incapable of handling herself or controlling her dark thoughts. On those days, she wished he had killed her instead of leaving her uncovered on the hard dry ground. Several questions rushed through her mind at each memory of the incident. In tears and anger she often asked, *"God, why did You allow this to happen to me? Where was Jesus when this happened to me? Why didn't He stop the attacker? Why doesn't He help me when I ask? Why me, Lord. Why me?"*

Seeing that God had said He would not allow her to take her life, she often begged God to just take her life from her because she would rather be dead than be feeling such intense heartache and abandonment. She often felt that God abandoned her, but it is written in Hebrews 13:5 (KJV), God promises *"I will never leave you nor forsake you."* God was always with Gloria, but she was too focused on her situation to even notice. Eventually, Gloria came to realize that God will not just give the answer like a counsellor would at that moment when she asked but she had to seek after God to know the plans He had for her why he did not allow her to die when she tried to kill herself. So she set out to do just that. She started by reading the bible daily, meditating on the word of God and praying again.

****

It took a while for Gloria to learn that regardless of how long it takes, help will come. God will send the help needed. However, if we decide to run from the help, then we would be running away from being healed. In her head, Gloria knew that without help, she would be reliving that night and its aftermath over and over for the rest of her life. So she decided to settle with one counsellor. In doing so Gloria began to heal. The process was slow but each day, little by little, Gloria's mind became free and she was in a good place. Counselling helped Gloria to begin to understand and accept that none of what happened to her was her fault. This was the message the counsellor often reiterated to her. Many persons may say that the victim puts themselves in that situation as fingers are oftentimes pointed at the victim. However, the victim of a crime should never be blamed for the evil actions of someone else.

For a long time Gloria was on the road to recovering. She was healing and getting back to a normal routine of being a teenager when suddenly she reverted to self-hate and blaming herself once again for the abuse.

After a while, Gloria gave up on going to counselling because she thought she was better and could handle things on her own. However, there was something Gloria did not share with her counsellor and this proved to be the open door that sent her back into a tailspin of depression.

Gloria had never opened up to any of her counsellors about her promiscuity. She kept that all to herself and now she was wrestling with that dark aspect of her life as thoughts of how used she was kept crowding her mind. Gloria knew she had to find a permanent fix to her fragmented mind because when she encountered triggers that reminded her of her past, she would fall into deep depression and began avoiding God. She would be reminded of the fact that God could have stopped the attacker, but He refused to and so she was done with Him.

While Gloria was still attending church, she was in a detached relationship with God. She tried hard never to connect or focus her mind on God while in church. She was afraid. Afraid that if she opened herself to God once again and went back to serving Him wholeheartedly as she did before, something bad would happen to her again. She lacked understanding of how amazing God is and what He is able to do for His children. What Gloria didn't realize was that there was purpose in all she endured. You may say, but how can purpose emerge from going through pain? But if you let go and let God you'll be amazed to see that in your pain is your purpose. The only prayer that Gloria prayed in the years since she stopped going to the counselor was the "Lord's Prayer", mostly as a recital. She was afraid to talk to God. In fact, she was more ashamed to do so because of all the things she had done after the abuse. On several occasions Gloria thought of how people may judge her and say all kinds of hurtful things to her if she ever spoke out about that part of her past. One thing is for sure is that unless we have walked a mile in someone else's shoes, we will never truly understand their hurt and pain and why they do the things they do.

Once Gloria stopped going to the counsellor, her emotions went back to being like a rollercoaster as she brooded over her behaviour. A desperate need for change grew deep inside her as she wanted to feel alive again. She wanted to laugh, be happy and enjoy her life to the fullest but was this possible for a girl who was so scarred? She didn't know the answer but she sure wanted it to be so.

****

Based on an invitation from a friend, Gloria visited a church and to her amazement the preacher's message was about letting go of the things that hurt us so that we can see God's plan for our lives. Though dazed, she listened attentively and held on to every word. By the end of the sermon Gloria felt a shift on the inside and memories of her past Christian life filled her thoughts. She remembered singing on the choir, leading praise and worship, giving welcome speeches, assisting with Sunday school and on occasions playing the instruments. A little smile lifted the corners of her lips as the pleasant memories invaded her thoughts. Gloria took a bold walk to the altar. The preacher looked at her as though he could see through her as she nervously stood with tears streaming down her face.

The preacher held on to her and prayed. Oh, how he prayed. The next thing she knew she was on the floor crying out to God. Gloria cried profusely while asking God to help her and to take the pain away from her. Since that day at the altar she has never been the same. She found herself wanting to and attending church more often. With each visit she would sit closer and closer to the front of the church. The sermons always captivated her and left her feeling more and more hopeful. One day she decided to try God again and with that decision Gloria confessed her sins, repented and made her peace with God.

With Gloria's renewed faith in God she began getting the answers to her questions and the strength needed to fight the monster that had plagued her mind for years. With this renewed relationship with God came the realization that God had always been with her and He had been with her that night. It was not God's will or her desire to be abused but the overriding will of someone else to abuse her. Being raped was not a punishment from God for something Gloria did or didn't do. It was the act of a cowardly predator who preyed on little children. As Gloria leaned more into God this knowledge became more apparent.

By leaning on God for strength, Gloria's faith became more solid. She knew God loved her dearly and in His love He had sent others in her life to help her. The help came in several ways, all she had to do was stretch out her hand and grasp the opportunity to utilize the support systems available. To lay her past life out in the open was not easy. It took a great deal of courage and boldness for her to do so. Despite it being difficult she always remembered that no man is an island and no man can stand alone. So she went for it and ***just do it***! She boldly accepted the help that was offered.

Once Gloria decided to accept the help she began working feverishly on getting herself better. Gloria talked to counsellors, read uplifting and inspirational books. She read the bible and did research on the internet to find ways of coping and overcoming the pain of her past. She started feeling like her old self again. .

As she matured in her mind she prayed and through prayer she was able to release her burdens. She kept a journal where she wrote her thoughts down especially when the memories of that night resurfaced and threatened to overwhelm her. Facing the reality of being raped is not easy. Getting over it is even harder but Gloria turned to God for comfort. The bible scripture that helped Gloria to understand that she was not to be blamed is **Deuteronomy 22:25-26 [NIV]** *"[25]But if out in the country a man happens to meet a girl pledged to be married and rapes her, only the man who has done this shall die. [26] Do nothing to the girl for she has committed no sin deserving death"*. Oh what comfort the words of God brought to her dry and desperate soul when others would seek to make her feel guilty. This scripture helped Gloria to realize that rape victims should not be blamed for what happened to them. Society may say that it is oftentimes the girl's fault because she dresses in an inviting way but this is not so. Even if a woman/girl attires herself in a particular way, it does not give anyone the right to abuse her. Thus such a statement is unfair and definitely not true and **Deuteronomy 22:25** made that clear.

Gloria did not dress provocatively as she was a young Christian girl who dressed modestly according to the teachings of her faith. [The Word of God says *"Know ye not that ye are the temple of God, and that the Spirit of God dwelleth in you?* (**1 Corinthians 3:16 KJV**).] Therefore, "If any man defiles the temple of God, him shall God destroy; for the temple of God is holy, which temple ye are" (**1 Corinthians 3: 17 KJV**). Armed with this knowledge she did everything to maintain her purity and her holiness. Despite this she was attacked. Gloria knew it was not God's will for bad things to happen to her but she accepted the fact that as Christians we go through trials and tribulations. This helped her to fight when darkness wanted to engulf her.

Combating the memories of trauma is a war, a battle and you will have to put up a fight. As the lingering thoughts of the incident continued to torment Gloria, she made a decision based on what is written in **Ephesians 6:11 KJV**, *"put on the whole armour of God, that ye may be able to stand against the wiles of the devil".* Gloria was learning that the torture faced during or after a traumatic situation is a device used by the devil to get our minds off God and to focus on the situation. When your mind is not on God then you will not be able to see the purpose God has for your life. We are hindered by the obstacles the devil place in our lives to distract us.

With Gloria becoming more spiritually mature she was able to speak to her flashbacks and take authority over her life. Her situation could no longer hurt her because she had taken dominion over it being mindful of **Romans 6:14** that says *"... sin [or trauma] shall not have dominion over you: for ye are not under the law, but under grace."*. With every flashback she decided that enough was enough and she spoke with authority as she hardened her heart.

"Ok, there you go just play out, are you done?" As the thoughts faded she whispered *"Satisfied? You can no longer hurt me. You cannot win. You have failed, I am stronger now"*.

Gloria smiled as she celebrated another victory over the scar. Yes, it is a scar. It will always be there but she will not let it affect who she is and who she wants to become. It's over. It's done. Halleluiah!

We have to constantly remember that *"the Lord is a stronghold for the oppressed, a stronghold in times of trouble"* (**Psalm 9:9 ESV**), so no matter how you feel at any given time, just remember God is with you. You may never forget what happened but you can get over it. It will not be easy but it is time for you to be a victor and not a victim. Gloria remained a victim up until her recommitment with God because she allowed the thoughts of her past to consume her. The persons who hurt you have the power over you as long as you hold onto the hurt. In holding onto the hurt you cannot see your prevailing destiny that is ordained for you. You are destined for greatness and you will not begin to fully live and enjoy life until you first accept what happened, forgive your abuser and yourself and connect with God.

Gloria spent all those years struggling with the pain and hurt because she had not yet found the right solution for her problem. Yes, she sought out several avenues to get help but her mind was not on the Most High God, the only true healer for all such circumstances and situations. **Matthew 6:33** (KJV) reminds us that when we *"seek first the kingdom and His righteousness, and all these things shall be added to you"*. Therefore, if you seek after God you will find Him and He will give you the desires of your heart. Do not wait until it's too late before the right avenue is sought for your mind to be freed from the prison of bad experience. Bear in mind that *"they that wait upon the Lord shall renew their strength, they shall mount up with wings as eagles; they shall run, and not be weary; and they shall walk, and not faint* (**Isaiah 40:31** KJV). Seek and find that strength you need to mend the broken vessels of your heart that can only be found in God Almighty.

Like Gloria, many persons who have been abused are often stuck in their pain because they lean on their own understanding. If Gloria had gotten the help she needed immediately after the incident, she would have had it a lot easier. If she had shared her experience with others – a parent, school counselor, pastor or close friend - she would have gotten the help she needed to free her mind. She was held captive for years because she was lost in her situation. Do not be lost in your situation. Living a life of pain and hurt cannot be the solution you seek. Get up! Rise up! Take a stance now and find a solution to your problem with God's help.

On many occasions we may think that the people who hurt us are getting off "scotch-free" but let us remember **Romans 12:19 (KJV)** that says *"Dearly beloved, avenge not yourselves, but rather give place unto wrath: for it is* *written, Vengeance is mine; I will repay, saith the Lord. Therefore, "Do not say, "I will repay evil"; wait for the Lord, and He will deliver you"* (**Proverbs 20:22 ESV**). Additionally, it is written, *"Grace be to you, and peace, from God our Father, and from the Lord Jesus Christ"* (**Ephesians 1:2 KJV**). Remember, *"Ye [you] are of God, little children, and have overcome them, because greater is He that is in you, than he that is in the world* (**1 John 4:4 KJV**), *for whatsoever is born of God overcomes the world. And this is the victory the world – our faith"* (**1 John 5:4 KJV**). Be confident that you will overcome. Even though you may feel so drained you think you do not have the ability to fight your situation, you may not even know what to do. But have you ever thought of praying?

By focusing all your attention on God through prayer and reading His word, you will find solace. God is able to do the abundantly, exceedingly, great things that will transform your life but you have to ask Him. As **1 John 5: 14-15 (KJV)** states *"Now this is the confidence that we have in Him that if we ask anything according to His will, He hears us. And if we know that He hears us, whatever we ask, we know that we have the petitions that we have asked of Him."*

Go ahead and ask your Heavenly Father for the desires of your heart. God alone can mend the broken pieces of your life. He alone can rearrange the puzzles and make your life better. Through all her struggles, Gloria learned that it hurts more when she let the situation control her. Do not let your situation control you. Pull yourself together. It is not over and will never be over unless you give up on trying. Now is not the time to give up on you. Remember your purpose? The one intended for you by our Heavenly Father? Dive deeper into God's word so that your purpose can be clearer to you and use it to keep you going.

Let us use Gloria's situation, if there was no purpose for her to fulfill, don't you think she would have died given the number of times she tried to kill herself? Everything she tried failed. You may look at your situation now and say to yourself *"**There is no way out of it.**"*
But rise up as the warrior you are and take a stance knowing that *"The thief (enemy) cometh not, but for to steal, and to kill, and to destroy: I (the Lord) am come that they might have life, and that they might have it more abundantly"* (**John 10:10 KJV**). So *"Be sober, be vigilant because your adversary the devil, as a roaring lion, walketh about, seeking whom he may devour"* (**1 Peter 5:8 KJV**). Use these scriptures to start your

journey to finding your purpose, to finding your true self, the one God created you to be. Your destiny is promised unto you and the devil will stop at nothing to ensure that you do not achieve your full potential so you have to fight. Always remember you are a part of God's designed plan. You are not an accident. So live within the design that God has for your life by first *"submit[ting] yourselves therefore to God, resist the devil and he will flee from you"* (**James 4:7 KJV**). Do not let the devil have dominion over you and stifle your destiny, your God given purpose.

Have you ever read the scriptures or watched the movies that portrayed the bible story of Jesus' preparation for the crucifixion? If you have not, I recommend you watch the ***"Passion of the Christ"***. This movie gives a true depiction of what Christ went through for us. The bible tells us that Jesus was brutally beaten under the watchful eyes of the people who loved Him as well as those who hated Him. He was tortured and I am sure that the human side of Him must have wanted to give up and ask God to deliver Him from all the pain. Even as the nails pierced His body, He endured it. Why did He do all of that? He did it for us so that our sins can be forgiven and ultimately for the completion of His purpose on earth. You may be thinking, *"But what does that have to do* *with all of what I am going through?"* Your situation has a purpose embedded in it just as Jesus' did. You may not see the purpose because you are blinded by your circumstance but **all things work together for God's purpose**.

There is hope for you and it is possible to find back your place in God. *"But the God of all grace, who hath called us unto his eternal glory by Christ Jesus, after that ye have suffered a while, make you perfect, stablish, strengthen, [and] settle you"* (**1 Peter 5:10 KJV**) is a promise made to you and I. We just have to believe and never lose sight of it.

Gloria never knew that healing would come, but it did. Why? Because she learned to let go and let God as **1 Peter 5:7 (KJV)** states *"cast all your care upon Him; for He care[s] for you."* and **1 Peter 4:16-19 (KJV)** tells us that:

> *… if any man suffer as a Christian, let him not be ashamed; but let him glorify God on this behalf. For the time is come that judgement must begin at the house of the God; and if it first begin at us, what shall the end be of them that obey not the gospel of God? And if the righteous scarcely be saved, where shall the ungodly and the sinner*

appear? Wherefore let those that suffer according to the will of God commit the keeping of their souls to him in well doing, as unto a faithful creator.

Oh what a reassurance that is for people who have been hurt or are experiencing challenges. In many instances it takes a situation or a circumstance for us to know that God still exists. Sometimes it is the trauma that we face in our lives that causes us to return to God. Many persons would not have known their strength and true ability to excel if they had not been on their faces, burdened with problems.

Gloria used her experience of being raped to counsel young girls that have been raped. It was not something that she had ever thought of doing but it is quite evident it was a part of her purpose. When girls would open up to Gloria about being raped she was often dumbfounded because she could not understand how it is that they saw her as a person to talk to about something that she took almost a year to talk about. Amidst the pain of her situation, she was able to help those girls. Often times the girls send thank-you messages to her, thanking her for her help and encouragement during their difficult time. You may be wondering how it is that someone who was so deep in pain and hopelessness could help others? It was her purpose. Gloria began to look at the list of girls that had opened up to her and began to see one of her purposes. She realized she was called to minister to young girls and women out of her experience.

It is amazing how much you can help someone who is in a similar situation. Some people may say you are not the best person to assist someone else with a similar situation, but who else is able to do it better than the person who has lived it and overcame it. The fact is both Gloria and the girls were benefitting from the conversations. While it provided healing for the girls it was therapeutic for Gloria as well. As she spoke to each of the girls she was also speaking to herself.

It was difficult at first when she began counselling them because her mind was not healed entirely and the memory of the experience brought her pain. Each time she recounted aspects of her experience to help the girls, the feelings associated with the rape tried to resurface after the counselling sessions. Gloria had no idea how she found the strength and the knowledge to say the right words of encouragement to the young girls, but she believed that the Holy Spirit was working through her. The more girls she counselled the more she realized that the situation could have been much worse for her.

There are some persons who did not survive being sexually abused because either the attacker killed them or they killed themselves. She had not gotten pregnant and had not contracted any sexually transmitted diseases. Sometimes it may take someone else's situation to breathe a sense of relief over your circumstance. You may have had only one encounter of rape, but there are girls who are living it daily. They are raped every day and they can't seem to find a way out of it.

For those who have had a child as a result of the attack or have contracted a disease, all hope is still not lost. Remember that the child is innocent in all of this. Children are a blessing even though the child came into the world in such a painful situation. God still has a purpose for that child.

The Bible says that love covers a multitude of sins. If it is that you have contracted a disease then put your faith to the test and believe that Jesus Christ is the greatest physician and nothing is impossible for Him. He can heal you of your disease if you have faith. **Hebrews 13:1** says *"Now faith is the substance of things hoped for, the evidence of things not seen."* Turn to Him and He will give you the desires of your heart. Nothing is too big for God to do. You may feel that your struggle is unique, but always remember that it is not. There is someone somewhere who has faced, or is facing what you are experiencing. The devil likes to have us believe that what we are going through is unique to us to get us isolated and depress but do not believe that lie. You are never alone. There is always someone you can talk to who can help you get through your pain. You too will have a Gloria to share your feeling with. God is able to do anything once we surrender to His will and His ways. Let God help you. Let Him heal your broken heart. Here is a simple prayer that can help you get started:

PRAYER

"Lord, I know I have been living a life of hurt and pain for so long but I am ready to be set free. I am ready to lay it all on your shoulders. Father, as Your word says we should cast our cares upon You because You care for us... so I give all my fears, hurt, pain and worry to You. Please help me to be a new creature in You. Help me to know You more and to seek You. Help me to understand that I am wrapped and tied up in Your greatness and I must achieve that which You have destined over my life. Help me to understand that I am Your child and I have Your DNA so failure is not an option.

Father, please forgive me for leaning unto my own understanding and not leaning on You for comfort. I am great, I am blessed and highly favoured. I am no longer in bondage. I am free. Thank you Jesus I am free. Free at last, I am free at last. Thank God almighty I am free in Jesus name. Amen."

Now that you have prayed the prayer to God, do not leave it there. Seek after Him through constant prayer and reading the word. Also, if you are not already attending a spirit filled church that teaches the word of God, do so in order for your spirit to be fed with word. It was while listening to a powerful preacher that Gloria got back on track to accomplishing her purpose. While in a service the preacher said *"God cannot change you if he doesn't own you. If God has your life, He has everything. You cannot be blessed until God sits in your life and direct the affairs of your life. God blesses those who He uses."* As Gloria pondered on these words, she knew exactly what she had to do to get over the hurt and pain she was going through. She decided to live for God and lay all her burdens on Him. She decided to live a life free of pain and full of worth and purpose.

God has a plan for each of our lives and the devil will try to block those plans by orchestrating his intentions to bring you down and get your mind off God and by extension your own abilities and goals. The plan of God is not to hurt or harm you. In fact, through your pain, hurt and struggles, you may see opportunities that will guide you to your purpose.

There was a point in time when Gloria could not believe in any of these things about purpose or God's plan for her life. She always thought "what purpose could I fulfill being so battered and bruised?" We all at some point in our lives think less of ourselves because of the situations we have encountered. You are a child of God and always remember *"God has not given us the spirit of fear; but of power, and of love, and of a sound mind"* (**2 Timothy 1:7**). Bear in mind that in your purpose driven life the enemy, the devil, will stop at nothing to take your focus off the Most High God.

The fact of being raped or abused in whatever form is painful to deal with. Like everything else in life, the pain is just for a season. That season of hurt will come to an end, but you must make the right decisions as it relates to seeking the help you need in order to reach that place of freedom. *"So if the Son (Jesus Christ) sets you free, you will be free indeed* (**John 8:36**).

When you are stuck in the midst of your struggles you may think that there is no way out of this situation that you are facing. But have you stopped a minute to think about the plans you had for your life and how the turmoil you are now faced with is a setback to your progress? Be free from your past and dive into the life that has been set out for you. It is for freedom that Christ has died for you. *"Stand firm, then, and do not let yourselves be burdened again by a yoke of slavery [pain]"* (**Galatians 5:1 NIV**). Unless you escape from being a slave in your own body, mind and spirit, you will be stuck in your present situation.

In order to be completely free you must first of all forgive yourself. Many times the first person we blame is ourselves. It was my fault why this happened to me. Is it though? Did you ask someone to hurt you deliberately? Think about it, why should you be blamed for someone else's actions? If your adult child misbehaves the parents are often blamed for how the child was raised but after all isn't everyone responsible for their own behaviour? Don't pin yourself down with the sin of someone else. Think a little about the pain you are presently feeling or have felt. Is it really something you want to be holding on to? Is it a feeling that you want to have every second of every day? It may be hard now and the desperation to get rid of the pain may increase.

You may have questions of how to move from your present mind-set.   I recommend that you begin by speaking positively over yourself, your life and your situation. Do you remember what Gloria did when the flashbacks came? She spoke with authority that her situation could no longer hurt her because she had taken dominion over it. She spoke boldly. It could not win; it had failed because she was stronger. You know that could have not been easy for her to speak to the flashbacks as they reminded her of the pain she endured. It may not be easy for you either to speak contrary to what you are feeling but you have to push and focus on the healing that you want to have.

As promised in **Isaiah 61:1** the Spirit of the Sovereign Lord is on [you] and He will bind up your broken heart and give you freedom. You are a prisoner to your past and until you release yourself and take back authority over your life, you will not escape the place you are now in. A better life is promised to all of God's children. God's promises are true and He said He will never leave you nor forsake you.

Even in your worst situations, He is there. He is guiding you through. Even though you may feel down and out now and think that God has somehow forgotten or abandoned you, He hasn't. The Apostle Paul wrote in the book of **Philippians 4:19** that "… *my God will meet all your needs according to the riches of his glory in Christ Jesus."* God will deliver you out of all that you are facing. Just trust in Him and believe that He will see you through.

Like Gloria did before she got deliverance, you may have blamed God for your present situation but you will not see the blessing that may be present in the midst of what you are facing. Your struggles are not meant to kill you but to make you stronger. Gloria learnt overtime that what she went through was not for her but for the people God will use her to help. There are persons waiting on you to overcome so that they can be guided to freedom with your help. Trust in God and lean on Him for comfort. **Romans 8:28** reminds us that God causes everything to work together for the good of those who love God and are called according to his purpose for them. With all the promises given to you by the supreme God and Saviour, do you still want to hold on to your past?

The only result of holding on to pain and hurt is more pain, hurt and misery. You need to make a decision today to follow the Lord so that He can fulfil His desires in you. *"May the God of hope fill you with all joy and peace as you trust in him, so that you may overflow with hope by the power of the Holy Spirit"* (**Romans 15: 13 NIV**). Know too that they that wait upon the lord shall renew their strength. They will [soar] on wings like eagles; they will run and not grow weary, they will walk and not faint (**Isaiah 40:31 KJV**).

So come on, rise up from that state of mind, renew your strength in the Lord and get ready to fulfil the dream that God has planned out for you. Titus prayed to God thanking him for His grace that brought salvation unto him; teaching him to deny ungodliness and worldly lusts and live soberly, righteously and godly as he look for that blessed hope in the Father and Jesus Christ our Saviour glorious appearing, in Jesus name (**Titus 2:11-13 KJV**).

Like Titus, let your prayer be that of thanksgiving, for the saving grace of our Lord Jesus Christ who came to die for our sins so that we may be saved and be set free from bondage. Pray that God will show you a way out of your current state of being. It is not worth wasting your future because of your past. The past is only alive in your mind because you are holding on to it. The moment you release it you will have a sense of freedom to live your life in accordance with the will of God. Decide in your heart to seek after God in order to have a relationship with Him and see the transformation that will happen in your life. The power your pain and past have over you will melt away like snow on a hot day. It just takes total surrendering to God.

CHAPTER FOUR: LIVING THE PREDESTENED DREAMS

Now that you have gone through the previous chapters, you should be at a place, where you can reflect on and start believing the words of God. You should have already made a decision in your heart to give your burdens to the Lord. You must now be in a state of mind that is ready to push through to the next level which is living the life that is already planned for you. Be open as you prepare your mind, spirit, soul and body for what lies ahead of you.

In all that has happened there is still life, and once there is life, there is hope. God has given us hope for a better tomorrow. So if a better tomorrow is promised, why stay stuck in the past? Praise be to God, Gloria was set free from her past and is now living a purpose filled life. How would you feel if your life is a blessing to someone else's? It can be, but you first have to be set free and be in a place of peace.

Though your past may not be forgotten, God will grant you His peace. A peace that is guaranteed through seeking after Him. After you seek and find the Lord He will grant you the desires of your heart coupled with His will for your life. Gloria may never forget the horrors of her past life, but with the peace given to her through Christ Jesus, she is made whole. She can now use her past life as a testimony to pull someone else out of their situation. You too may not forget the things that you have been through, but know that what you went through may just help you to pull someone else out of a similar situation. The memories allow you to remember where you were and the gratitude of overcoming all your past challenges should be a springboard to reach out to someone else.

As you move away from your life of misery, remember to put God at the head of your life and everything else will fall into place. With God as the head of Gloria's life she forgave all the people that caused her hurt and pain and even herself for holding onto the pains for so long. You may think that you cannot forgive the person or people that caused you pain, but Jesus is the solution to any problem. And with his strength you can do anything. Isaiah 40:29 tells us that *He gives power to the weak, And to those who have no might He increases strength.* Know that no matter what you go through in this life once you have Jesus and believe in what He can do for you, the victories will be yours. God says in **Isaiah 41:10 (ESV),** *"fear not, for I am with you; be not dismayed, for I am your God; I will strengthen you, I will help you, I will uphold you with my righteous right hand."*

Many persons may be afraid of moving on because they are afraid of what lies ahead. But why should you? Leap out and grab unto your dreams and make them manifest. The goodness of God will remain with you and He will grant you the strength you need to be victorious. Remember that every situation or circumstance in your life is preparing you for the life you have ahead. You will begin to feel the need to do things that you never thought that you could do, but God has a plan for you from the day you were conceived. **Jeremiah 1:5** states that *"Before I [God] formed you in the womb I knew you, and before you were born I consecrated you; I appointed you a prophet to the nations."* The Lord God knew you from before you were conceived and henceforth His plan for your life was written. With this knowledge you should be excited about your future.

So give joyful thanks to the Father, who has qualified you to share in the inheritance of His holy people in the kingdom of light. For He has rescued (you) from the dominion of darkness and brought (you) into the kingdom of the Son He loves, in whom we have redemption, the forgiveness of sins (**Colossians 1:12-16**). *He also gives power to the weak and strength to the powerless. Even youths will become weak and tired, and young men will fall in exhaustion. But those who trust in the Lord will find new strength. They will soar high on wings like eagles. They will run and not grow weary. They will walk and not faint* (**Isaiah 40:29-31 NLT**).

You may not know what your purpose in life is yet, but do you really want to sit around and wonder? Or would you rather seek after God to discover His given purpose for you? Seeking after God and allowing Him to show you the plans He has for you is the only way to start living a rewarding and satisfying life. Being dead in a situation for so long may place your mind in a place of confusion. A place where you are not sure about what exactly you ought to be doing. If this is your case, then think back to the years before all the misery started in your life and remember the dreams you had then. We have all in our formative years dreamed of the life that we wanted and though situations may have stunted those dreams, it is not the end of it. Get a vision board and write those early visions you had for yourself down. Use pictures to show the life you wanted to live before your troubles started. Little by little start working on achieving each item on the board. You see, God has already laid out His plans for you. In **Jeremiah 29:11 (NIV)** the Lord says, *"For I know the plans I have for you. They are plans for good and not for disaster but to give you a future and a hope."* Rest assured that God is the same yesterday, today and forevermore and He will never go back on His words. *"God is not a man, so he does not lie. He is not human, so he does not change his mind. Has He ever spoken and failed to act? Has he ever promised and not carried it through?"***(Numbers 23:19 NLT)**

The Lord will fulfil His promises in your life. But in order for God to make His plans manifest, you will have to surrender to His will and to His ways. The Lord says in **Isaiah 55:8 (KJV),** *"for my thoughts are not your thoughts, neither are your ways my ways."* The Lord knows what it is that He wants you to do but how will you know if you do not have a relationship with Him? Would a complete stranger release personal information to you without first building a relationship with you where they can trust you to hear and accept what they have to say? Well, God knows everything about you and He wants to share the plans He has for you with you, but first you have to develop that relationship with Him where you trust Him and He trusts you to do His will.

But how can I do that, you may ask? Begin by talking to God, reading and meditating on His words. God is able to make all crooked path straight and He will reveal to you that which you are called or chosen to do in this life.

In **Psalm 138:8 (ESV)** David said that *"the lord will fulfil his purpose for me, your steadfast love, O lord, endures forever. Do not forsake the work of your hands."* The Lord fulfilled His purpose for David and He will do the same for you. You will not be able to see that which you were born to accomplish if your mind is not in the right place. **Romans 12:2 (ESV)** says that you should *"not be conformed to this world, but be transformed by the renewal of your mind, that by testing you may discern what is that will of God, what is good and acceptable and perfect."* With that said, if you haven't done that already, think about refocusing your mind today.

Don't worry about the lost years, think about that which is in front of you and believe that all things will work out for you. It is written in **Romans 8:28 (KJV)** that *"all things will work together for good for those who love God and those who are called according to His purpose."* The promise is also for you, but you have to love the Lord and seek after Him with all your heart so that His will can be made manifested in your life.

Remember Gloria and where she was in her mind? But you know what? She found God and is living the dream that was predestined for her by the Creator, through the saving grace of the Lord Jesus Christ. That can also be you.

You wanted to give up on your life because of the pain you felt. Why not give up on the past now and focus on the future. The past does not matter once you are under the lordship of Jesus Christ, the one who died so that we can have life and have it more abundantly. **Philippians 4:13** assures you that you can do all things through Christ who gives you strength. So go ahead and take that step today.

I pray that *"out of his glorious riches he may strengthen you with power through his Spirit in your inner being. So that Christ may dwell in your hearts through faith. And I pray that you, being rooted and established in love"* **(Ephesians 3: 16-17 NIV)**, will walk in your purpose. What does it really take to live a life that is already planned out, already destined for you? You may not know what it is that God has in store for you. But do you want to sit and think of what your life would have been like if you haven't gone through past hurts and past situations which are already gone? What gain in there in doing that? It is the past. What's in the past should stay in the past as you look forward on the things that you want to accomplish, the things you want to achieve. Start now. Paul says in **Philippians 3:13** *"Brethren, I do not count myself to have apprehended; but one thing I do, forgetting those things which are behind and reaching forward to those things which are ahead."*

You may have wanted to attend university, start a business or whatever dreams you had and you thought you could not do it because of your past situation or your circumstance. But I encourage you, like Paul forget the past and begin to reach for those dreams today.

As stated in the beginning of this book, the stories recounted are the real life experienced of a girl who was raped, became wounded and self-destructive, lost hope, became promiscuous in an effort to erase her past. She felt she had lost the one chance she had to become successful. But that was not the case. You see, I am Gloria. I did all the things I am advising you to do and they worked. Today I am a successful business woman with a noble profession.

There was a point in time when I gave up most of the things that I wanted to do because I was told that I could not do them. I often heard from people close to me, Who are you to do this? Who are you to do that? But God had placed certain desires in my heart and if i didn't follow through with them then I wouldn't be the person I am today. Yes, I was raped, I had financial struggles, yes, I grew up in a life that I thought could have been better but after a while I appreciated the struggles and the setbacks I had gone through. The thing is, it only lasted for a season. It is the same for you. It is only for a season and even if that season lasted longer than you want it to, it will pass eventually.

I never knew that I had the desire to do these things and it was when I overcame the hurtful past that I found who I really was in Christ Jesus. It may hurt for a while but it will not last forever. You have to take that stance, you have to make that decision and say enough is enough. I am taking back my destiny. I am taking back my God given purpose. You have the right but do you have the will do it?

You may not see it as yet but I want to suggest to you that what you are going through is all a part of your purpose. You will see it after you have overcome your situation. Out of being raped, I was able to help others who were going through a similar situation. I wrote this book you are now reading to share my story of hope and victory in Jesus Christ. Sit down in the presence of the Lord, talk to Him, and ask Him to let His purpose and plans for your life be manifested. Ask Him to show you what are His plans. There are so many things that you can achieve in this life because you already have all of that you need embedded inside of you to be victorious

Greatness is already inside of you. It is right there waiting for you to unlock it. Situations or circumstances that you face in life may temporarily mask the plans that God has for you but they are still there. You have the ability to make a change and live the life you desire. I did it and you can do it too. You may ask, how can I get over this? Begin with the renewal of your mind. Speak to yourself, speak to your situation. There is power in the tongue. When God was creating this earth, he spoke "Let there be light and there was light, let there be a firmament in the heavens and on earth." He spoke it. He said what He wanted and it happened. You may say that is God He has the power to do so, but we also have the power to speak things into being because His Word declares in **Proverbs 18:21KJV** *"Death and life are in the power of the tongue, And those who love it will eat its fruit."*

Speak life into your situation daily and the change you desire will manifest. You will have to put in the work and the effort needed, but at least you are speaking into yourself, you are speaking to your situation. In speaking to yourself, your faith will increase and you will have the courage to leap out, to launch out and work on the plans and desires you have for yourself. Come on. Think of all the people you could have been helping with that dream that you have. A dream is only dead if you let it. I usually hear the elderly folks say that you can carry a cow to the water but you can't force it to drink it. The same applies to your dreams. No one can force you to live your dreams but you. Whatever the profession that you want to venture into, God can use you and will use you in His own special way. You have a purpose. When will you realize that purpose? Why would you want to waste what God has given to you. Why?

You may be comparing your experience to others and wondering why it happened to you. Why didn't it happen to someone else? Why me? But think about it. Why is it only with negative things we ask the why question? If someone gave you a million dollars, would you say why me? Or would you just take it and thank the Lord for it? There is a purpose in every situation. A reason why everything happened.

Think back on all the things that I went through, it may not have been as devastating as yours but why would you compare or measure the degree of someone else's hurt? The word hurt is spelt the same way regardless of how you measure it. From what you have read so far you know I could have said, you know what I am giving up because this happened to me. But irrespective of what I went through I persevered.

Now, I am at a point in my life where I thank God for all the struggles that I went through and that takes great courage to be thankful for the negative situations you faced. But guess what? You can be thankful too. If you are still going through that situation and it seems hopeless, remember God is always with you. You can get out of it. Don't let your situation dominate you. Take charge of your life. You know what you want. So go and get it. God will see you through every situation. He says to call upon Him when you are not strong, so call upon Him and He will give you rest. Call upon Him and He will answer you.

Call upon Him and He will take you out of every dead situation. God is powerful. He is awesome. There is nothing my God, your God, our God cannot do. Put the enemy to shame. Find out today what your purpose is if you are still unsure. Sit down in a quiet place and pray and think of the talents or gifts that you have. Is this the talent I want to develop? We all have talents and gifts and though we may not be aware of them or even be using them and they can be developed into something great, we have them. However, that will not happen unless your mental capacity has changed significantly. Jesus loves you with an everlasting love. He cares for you. He sent his son to die for you. He gave you His only begotten son so that you might and will be saved. If it is that God sent His son to die so that your pains can be taken from you, then cast your burdens upon Him because He cares for you.

In **Philippians 4:19 (KJV)** Paul said to the people *"[that] my God shall supply all your needs according to his riches in glory by Christ Jesus."* God will also supply your needs, but you have to make God your desire. *"But seek first the kingdom of God and His righteousness, and all these things shall be added to you"* (**Matthew 6:33NKJV)**. Real and true comfort comes to you when you seek God and make Him the head of your life. With Him directing the affairs of your life, things will begin to fall into place. Will it always be easy? No it will not. Struggles will come but God will give you His grace to overcome any of the enemy's schemes. *"No temptation* *has overtaken you except such as is common to man; but God is faithful, who will not allow you to be tempted beyond what you are able, but with the temptation will also make the way of escape, that you may be able to bear it"* **(1 Corinthians 10:13NKJV).**

If you have not done so as yet, just make the decision right now to surrender to God. He will give you His peace. **John 14:27 (KJV)** says *"Peace I leave with you, my peace I give unto you: not as the world gives, give I unto you. Let not your heart be troubled, neither let it be afraid."* John has spoken about the peace of God in **John 16:33** when he says that *in me (Jesus) you may have peace. In the world you will have tribulation. But take heart, I (Jesus) have overcome the world. "I am leaving you with a gift—peace of mind and heart. And the peace I give is a gift the world cannot give. So don't be troubled or afraid"* **(John 14:27 NLT)**. With those promises from Jesus Christ, what are you waiting for? Go right ahead and live the life you were promised.

It is up to you now to move forward. You should be feeling motivated right now to get moving. Start with a plan for your life. You can make a list of all the things you want to accomplish and put a timeline to them. It is time to turn those dreams into goals and give each item on the list a realistic time when you want to achieve each goal. It does not matter how much time you may have wasted, it was all a part of your learning process. The fact that you are reading this book means that you are alive and have an opportunity to fix what was broken or neglected.

Many of what I have accomplished thus far are based on instructions from God that I acted on My desire to push beyond my earlier struggles of financial issues while attending high school gave me the intrinsic motivation to attend school because I wanted to fulfil my dream of becoming a teacher. With that drive I have acquired a teaching diploma, a bachelor's degree, and now pursuing a master's degree as well as an associate degree in biblical Studies. I am making my life count and it does not stop there as I will study until I die. I will go further up the academic, professional and spiritual ladders as I equip myself to be used by God.

Within a year of my transformed life I wrote twelve manuscripts and published a children's book called Hope. I have also started a publishing business. In my profession as a teacher, I use the opportunity to minister to the youths I interact with daily. In my current ministry at church I am the Children's Ministry Director at

Worship and Faith International Fellowship where I continue to impact young minds. Out of my past, I developed a passion to see the children grow with confidence in self and in God so they can impact God's kingdom and by extension the world positively. I cannot do it alone and you may just be the one God has chosen to help to make an impact as He directs you.

Do not be afraid to dream big and remember your dreams should influence your goals and you should set timelines. Do not worry about what people will say about you. That does not matter. What matters is that you are living your life according to God's blueprint. The greatest reward is the knowledge that God chose to use you for His glory and His honour. With such a privilege bestowed to you it is only necessary for you to use it.

I am joyfully serving the Lord and He is waiting on you to do the same. He loves you and has great plans for you. Always remember that all you need is in Him, There is peace and joy in Him. Prosperity is in Him. There is no lack in Him. Whatever you need is in Him. All you need to do is seek after Him and when you do you are guaranteed to be refreshed in Him. If you need peace check Him. You need an answer? Call on Him. Lost? Follow Him. What do you need? Ask Him. Restoration is in Him. Healing is in Him. Do not wait, I implore you today to run after Him and you will find Him. I have found Him and you will too.

God bless you on your pursuits to live a grand life in Jesus Christ. As you travel on your journey remember to take someone else with you. Help someone to find their purpose and live their life to the fullest.